THE VALUE OF HONEST MONEY

Published by

Appenzeller Business Press

NOTE ON SOURCES: Q&A sidebars are from the World Gold Council, an organization formed in 1987 and funded by the world's leading gold mining companies with the aim of stimulating and maximizing the demand for, and holding of, gold.

Copyright 2007 © Appenzeller Business Press AG
ISBN: 1893958-15-9

DEDICATION

I would like to dedicate this book first to my mother and father, who instilled in me the Golden Rule, Do Unto Others as You Would Have Them Do Unto You. As I grew older I came to understand and abide by two powerful laws, which Rick Maybury now articulates in his writings – Do what you say you will do, and don't encroach upon the rights of others as you go about your daily affairs.

I must also take the time to thank my wife of 25 years, Linda, for being that rock that we all need at the more difficult times in life.

"How I Found Freedom in an Unfree World," written by the late Harry Browne, has been for many years, a major influence on my thinking and behavior. As the rate of change in the world around us intensifies and problems seem to mount, I find that still another motto, "Prepare for the worst, but expect the best" helps keep me grounded, balanced and optimistic about the future. The book you are reading is meant to speak to these beliefs and offer solutions based upon the application of enduring principles of behavior. I firmly believe that reflecting upon these suggestions, and then taking actions which fit your personal circumstances and goals, will help you to move decisively forward.

Portions of this book — including its major analytical core — appear in other books in this series and elsewhere in other forms. Some material may have been drawn from third party sources.

DISCLAIMER

Welcome to Appenzeller Press' special limited edition series, The Value of Honest Money. Appenzeller Press' customized "core books" are offered to advisors and financial entrepreneurs who wish to express their own investment perspective and opinions alongside recognized economic education. Appenzeller Press is selective about those with whom it works on a paid basis and attempts to ascertain that participants subscribe to the theories espoused in the core book. However Appenzeller Press does not endorse any advisor or investment opportunity, nor intend to make any representations regarding the competence of a participant in its series. Additionally, Appenzeller Press does not intend to suggest that placement of the financial entrepreneur or company in a core book program provides any assurance of potential gains for clients. The prewritten core book is customized in consultation with the advisor and portions appear throughout the series. Participants contributions vary from five percent of the completed book to over 30 percent or more. Past performance is no guarantee of future results.

CONTENTS

INTRODUCTION

Let's begin at the beginning. We are in the grip of a financial crisis that threatens to wipe out the savings of millions of middle and upper middle class people, and if you don't know about it or don't understand, then you are in grave financial danger. If you have significant savings in US dollars in the form of cash, deposits and securities, then you run the risk of rapid asset degradation. This includes blue chip stocks and even American Treasuries.

Money is not what it once was. People used to exchange silver and gold coins for goods; today people use notes from central banks. While this does not seem on the surface to be an earthshaking change, in fact

the way people conceive of money today is far different than what money was understood to be years ago.

Today, the primary generator of money is the central bank in the Western world. A central bank is in charge of issuing "money" — paper bills — backed by the full faith and credit of the issuing country. By severing the link between precious metals and paper money, the West has embarked on a grand experiment that can only end in disaster, as it has countless times before. In China alone, in a 10,000 year history, there have been a number of fiat money episodes, and not a single one has lasted.

HONEST MONEY VERSUS FIAT

Without a linkage between an underlying asset and paper money, central bankers and politicians who also supervise

> *What is the history of honest money?*
>
> Honest money is a term that describes the direct use and circulation of silver and gold — money metals.

monetary policy, have removed many of the restraints that previously kept the generation of money in check. Now central banks can print as much money as they want, and all they have to fear is inflation — the result of printing too many notes and generating too much credit. But monetary inflation is a funny thing. It may not show up right away, or may be diverted and even subdued for long periods of time. The danger lies in a sudden outbreak of violent inflation that cannot be tamed.

For this reason, bank notes have come to be known by free-market economists as "fiat money." Gold and silver, on the other hand, are known as "honest money," because their value cannot be debased without physically attacking the coin or bar.

What's going on in today's world, which is full of fiat money? I call it "fiat evaporation." But it doesn't have to affect you. By showing you what I have done for myself and my family, as well as for thousands of other families with whom I have consulted over the years, I believe I can provide you with a plan to secure your assets even in the most tumultuous times.

There are little known but highly effective investments out there that can provide you with tremendous upside potential at a time when the majority of people around you are sinking into financial ruin.

HERE'S A PLAN — FOR YOU

Do you want to go the same way? Do you feel hopeless and without a plan? Do you

For this reason, bank notes have come to be known by free-market economists as "fiat money." Gold and silver, on the other hand, are known as "honest money."

blame those who went before you? You can feel all these things, or you can take action. Reading this book is a first step. What you are about to find out in this book is what I, along with millions of others already know and understand. At the end of the day we must all accept personal responsibility in our lives for the decisions we make. This means having enough conviction to stand back and accept what is really happening and, equipped with sufficient knowledge, do something about it.

This book, therefore, is only as useful as you want it to be. The facts are not in dispute. In fact if I wanted to, I could have an index a mile long with a litany of publications that reflect what I am saying. But this is not that kind of book. It is written tersely, to be acted upon. A suggested reading list is included at the back of the book along with a list of websites that I find to be a great source of knowledge.

Read this book. It will give you a solid base of knowledge and the conviction to implement my wealth strategies. They've worked for millions of us and now they can work for you.

HISTORY OF GOLD AND SILVER

I want to make the case to you for holding silver and gold — honest money. Simply put, you should know that silver and gold are money metals of market choice, having evolved from a competition between various kinds of commodities. Silver and gold are malleable, portable and attractive. These precious metals don't decay and thus hold their value. They can be turned into coins that can be circulated easily and can take a lot of abuse without losing shape, color or luster.

Today, silver and gold remain a primary store of value even though many people in the West don't realize it. A long campaign of disinformation about silver and gold, culminating in first the outlawing of silver-as-money and then, later, the confiscation of gold

coins in the US and elsewhere has given people the idea that gold is a primitive form of exchange and that it has been superseded by paper currency and, more recently, by electronic transactions.

This book will make the case that such an interpretation profoundly misjudges the real value of gold and the way the real economy operates. Central banks, for instance, continue to hold gold in massive quantities. And in the near and Far East, gold has never lost its luster. Today, the Japanese are heavy gold buyers. And more individuals in the West are buying gold bullion, coins, ETFs, mining stocks or holding gold through a variety of derivative instruments.

Murray's Take on Money

Among modern economists, perhaps Murray Rothbard has written most simply and clearly about the history of money. Books like

> *What is Gold and why is its chemical symbol Au?*
>
> Gold is a rare metallic element with a melting point of 1064 degrees centigrade and a boiling point of 2808 degrees centigrade. Its chemical symbol, Au, is short for the Latin word for gold, 'Aurum', which literally means 'Glowing Dawn'. It has several properties that have made it very useful to mankind over the years, notably its excellent conductive properties and its inability to react with water or oxygen.

"What Has Government Done to Our Money?" explain how money matured in the West and how it changed in modern times.

To begin with, Rothbard points out, there was no money, only trade — the swapping of one kind of resource or valuable commodity for another. Eventually, one resource became a repository of value itself — salt, shells, gems, or precious metals such as silver or gold. Ultimately, gold became a leading repository of value for most of the ancient world. It was light, beautiful, malleable and serviceable. Silver, with many of the same properties, was a close runner-up. And throughout history, silver and gold have traded in a ratio with each other. People preferred it this way because if the ratio shifted dramatically, they knew that either the silver or gold circulating was likely debased. In this way, silver became the "commoners" money, while gold gradually assumed the role of money for a kingdom's "high finance."

Once silver and gold were established as money metals of choice, they were often stored in warehouses. And as these warehouses became more commonplace, they began issuing receipts to businessmen. These receipts could be used in place of silver and gold. They are what we know today as checks.

The monetary system, as man first constructed it, was relatively simple. Merchants perhaps, paid owners of warehouses for the convenience of storing "honest money."

Later on, warehouse owners began to lend out some of the fees they were gathering. The final evolution of the warehouse system saw the warehouse owner beginning to lend out quantities of silver and gold from his customers' stores. Today, this practice is known as fractional banking, and it is the source of continuing controversy among economists, especially hard—money economists.

Silver and Gold in the US

Silver and gold were available as money in the United States before the Civil War, but came under pressure afterward. First silver was taken out of circulation and, in the 1930s gold was, too.

People didn't much like the transition from silver and gold to "paper money." In fact, when Congress decided that silver could no longer be directly circulated as "money," farmers in the United States "heartland" were furious with this decision. They called it the "crime of 1876." They believed that the removal of silver as money gave an advantage to the Eastern establishment which would now more easily be able to buy up Western farmland and lock away resources and land assets. In fact, this is just what occurred.

In the 1930s, at the start of the Great Depression, Franklin Delano Roosevelt did to gold what Congress had already done with silver: He outlawed its circulation. Even today, the use of honest money is looked upon with great suspicion by the Federal authorities. "Money" has become what is printed by central banks (more about them in upcoming chapters). Thus, you and I — if we do not know better — keep most of our assets locked up in "paper" money. Such "money" was initially "bills" and could be presented to the US Federal Reserve for precious metals. Today, that option no longer holds. It took many centuries, but in the United States and most if not all of the rest of the Western world, honest money cannot be easily circulated.

In the next chapter we will examine how central banks gradually displaced honest money, and why.

Silver and gold — honest money — came into use after a free-market competition and were likely used for thousands of years as a basic medium of exchange.

HISTORY OF CENTRAL BANKING

In this chapter, we will learn about central banking, how it came about and why central banks seemingly give significant advantages to those closest to the "money spigot."

Let us review what we know to this point. Silver and gold — honest money — came into use after a free-market competition and were likely used for thousands of years as a basic medium of exchange. But as humans began to live in bigger and bigger groups, those who wanted more money and power began to think of ways to achieve these goals. Unfortunately, not all of the conclusions were scrupulous.

Sometimes, coins were "shaved" — a little bit of gold or silver was scraped off the coin, rendering it slightly less valuable. Private banks, for the most part, were not involved in such activities because banks depended on honorable reputations to stay in business. Thus, it was that non-bank individuals and unscrupulous businesspeople were involved at first in debasing coinage. But it must soon have become clear that the most profitable fraud needed to be leveraged by the issuance of money itself, and thus those at the very top of government became involved.

Development of Banking

To begin with, coins may have been deliberately mislabeled; over time the amount of precious metals in the coins gradually decreased. This was very common in the West and can be seen occurring in the Roman Empire and later as well.

> *How much gold is there in the world?*
>
> At the end of 2000, it is estimated that all the gold ever mined amounts to about 142,600 tonnes.

Around the 10th or 11th century, modern banking began to be developed, first in Venice and then elsewhere. Merchant banks provided wealthy individuals new ways of "making money with money." But as these banks spread from their Venetian home, new ways of generating income kept being developed. By the 15th century, private banks were being set up that shared the "faith and credit" of the government itself. This happened most notably in England where the ancestor of today's central bank was created as a way of helping England pay for its war debts.

What a central bank did is take the idea of issuing notes or bills to the next level. The king or emperor utilized the wealth of the state as the basis of the note issuance — printing paper that could be redeemed against the government's stores of precious metals. However, in practice the bills or notes were not usually redeemed, or not in such numbers as to create a run on the central bank. Instead, backed by the full faith and credit of the government, the central bank was able to print more paper than there was gold in its reserves. Over time, this much paper tended to depreciate in value, but the royal treasury gained full value on initial issuance.

Thus we see that the printing of paper money was an evolution of previous strategies to gain wealth for the state, starting with coin shaving and ending with the creation of the central banking process, also known as fractional banking.

Glorious Central Bank?

A host of socialist and quasi-socialist economists have glorified the role of central banks and obscured the real reason for their

invention. Perhaps the most brilliant of these central bank apologists was John Maynard Keynes, himself a central banker, whose great economic tract, "The General Theory of Employment, Interest and Money," advocated the use of both fiscal and monetary stimuli to make economies prosper.

Today, in the United States, the central bank is called the Federal Reserve System. While many aspects of the operations of the central bank are complex (one writer, William Greider, has called them "Secrets of the Temple"), the mechanism used by the central bank to

In simplest terms, central banks inflate by printing money. The more money they print, the cheaper money becomes, and the less a governments debt becomes.

inflate has likely remained unchanged from its inception.

In simplest terms, central banks inflate by printing money. The more money they print, the cheaper money becomes, and the less a governments debt becomes. By cheapening money, the government deprives individual citizens of part of the value of that money. As the value is eroded, the citizen becomes poorer, even if he or she doesn't notice it right away.

THREE WAYS CENTRAL BANKS OPERATE

There are three often-mentioned ways for central banks to help "stimulate" or "deflate" the economy.

One way is for the central bank to buy or sell Treasury IOUs.

Another way, which was more popular in the 18th and 19th centuries, is to raise and lower the rates of the so-called discount window, the amount that the central bank charges to its member banks for short-term borrowing.

The third way is to move short-term interest rates up or down.

The main manner in which central banks move the economy is by adding to or subtracting from the amount of money in circulation by buying or selling government bonds as mentioned above.

CENTRAL BANKS — THE REALITY

While the above mechanisms sound innocent in principle, in reality they all lead to the issuance of new money and credit into the economy, and thus debase what is already

in circulation — a mechanism that the media chooses to call "inflation."

But stripping away the fancy terminology and what is occurring with the issuance of new money and credit is a kind of tax, affecting holders of old money. Even raising short-term rates constitutes a kind of tax, because when rates are raised, bonds can lose their value, and citizens holding onto bonds, especially longer maturity bonds, can suddenly find themselves poorer by thousands of dollars as the market reacts to rate news.

While the manipulations of the central banking mechanism sound innocent enough, free-market economists fervently blame almost every economic disaster of the last 500 years, with the exception of Tulipomania, on government intervention in the money supply or the marketplace.

Where does the word Gold come from?

The word gold appears to be derived from the Indo-European root 'yellow', reflecting one of the most obvious properties of gold. This is reflected in the similarities of the word gold in various languages: Gold (English), Gold(German), Guld (Danish), Gulden (Dutch), Goud (Afrikaans), Gull (Norwegian) and Kulta (Finnish).

John Maynard Keynes himself, one of the leading apostles of central banking stated that not one man in a million actually understood the mechanism of inflation or the role that central banking played in it. For this reason, among others, Keynes was able to advance the idea that wage push was responsible for inflationary pressures.

How the Wealthy Benefit ...

Powerful private interests benefit from fiat-money disinflations and deflations just as they gain from a bank-induced boom. The wealth generation happens in several ways, though it is never widely reported, and certainly you won't see it on the nightly news.

One way that central banking benefits those who supervise them is by allowing access to new money and credit before it has trickled out into the general public. Since the central bank issues its debt-based "money" through commercial banks for the most part, these banks and those close to the banks get the benefit of new money before it has trickled out into the general economy.

By using money "first," those close to central banks get to use the money before it has been devalued via "inflation." Another way that people benefit is by being close to the regulatory apparatus — and understanding upcoming monetary policy. While such "understandings" may not constitute a crime, they certainly provide opportunities for clever operators to enrich themselves.

Of course, central banks are not presented in this way to the general public. Central banking is offered up on the news and in academia as necessary for the well-being of the average citizen's savings and

Central banking is offered up on the news and in academia as necessary for the well-being of the average citizen's savings and investments. Thus, the average person is not to be blamed for thinking that the economy could not get along without a central bank.

> **Why is gold measured in carats?**
>
> This stems back to ancient times in the Mediterranean/Middle East, when a carat became used as a measure of the purity of gold alloys. The purity of gold is now measured also in terms if fineness, i.e. parts per thousand. Thus 18 carats is 18/24th of 1000 parts = 750 fineness.

investments. Thus, the average person is not to be blamed for thinking that the economy could not get along without a central bank. Leave it to the experts, is still the attitude of most people. So long as pension plans are expanding, the stock market is going up and jobs are plentiful, individuals tend to believe that the economy is in good hands and that good, gray central bankers are working long hours on their behalf.

... AND YOU DON'T

When the market heads down, and the economy stutters, people take a different approach. They look around for someone to blame. Surprisingly, it is not usually central banks — because people don't understand the inflationary mechanism very well — but the politicians, corporations and others who have benefited from central banking money manipulations.

This is the beauty of the current central banking mechanism. It is very hard for you and me to figure out what they are without spending a great deal of time and energy. Even then, there is so much that supports central banking, it is very hard to arrive at a conclusion that is anti-central banking or that takes a position other than what is commonly accepted. That's one reason to read this book. I've taken the time to understand these issues. And in these pages, I'm sharing what I have learned with you.

HISTORY OF THE FEDERAL RESERVE

We've examined central banking's rise from a historical point of view. And in this chapter, we will focus even more closely on the rise of the American Federal Reserve and its historical roots, including banking episodes that should have put central banking into bad odor but did not.

We've already noted that central banking partakes of the "faith and credit" of central governments. In fact, it is most dangerous for such linkages to occur, as they paper over dangers and make people confident of taking risks that they would not otherwise take because they see governmental authority involved.

In fact, this process is not limited to central banking. Famous Wall Street trader

Victor Sperandeo traces some of these boom-bust occurrences in his book, "Methods of a Wall Street Master."

TWO GOVERNMENT BUSTS

In the following two examples, private interests utilized government power and the monopoly power of the government purse to create a financial disaster.

The Mississippi Bubble: In the case of the Mississippi Bubble, the blame can be laid at the feet of Scottish banker John Law. Because France had piled up a large debt under spendthrift King Louis XIV, Law succeeded in establishing a French central bank, the Banque Royale, whose purpose, among others, was to inflate away Frances debt. Later on, Law was able to form the Mississippi Company, which received exclusive trading rights in the Louisiana Territory and elsewhere

around the world. Law went public with stock in his company at the same time the French Central Bank was expanding the money supply. Much of the additional money was used by French citizens to buy stock in Law's company. And the money with which they purchased stock was used to pay off more of the French Crown's debt.

Eventually, it became clear that the Mississippi Company was not going to find the gold it had promised its shareholders. At the same time, the French government attempted to restrain the amount of gold and silver coins that French citizens could hold, because the Banque Royale had issued so much paper money that French citizens had

The Mississippi Company was not going to find the gold it had promised its shareholders. At the same time, the French government attempted to restrain the amount of gold and silver coins that French citizens could hold.

begun to convert their holdings into gold and silver.

A panic swept over French money markets, and the stock of the Mississippi Company collapsed. Because the central bank had issued so much paper money, the problem of the collapse of the Mississippi Company was compounded by a larger depression. Law lost at least part of his vast fortune and ended up leaving France. A council of bankers was formed, and it found that despite all the monetary stimulation, France's debts had actually increased during the time of the Banque Royale, and France was worse off than before.

The South Sea Bubble: Almost exactly the same scenario was played out in England during the episode that has come to be known as the South Sea Bubble. In this case, Robert Harley, Earl of Oxford, and scrivener John Blunt were given an international trading

What is a Carat?

A Carat (Karat in USA & Germany) was originally a unit of mass (weight) based on the Carob seed or bean used by ancient merchants in the Middle East. The Carob seed is from the Carob or locust bean tree. The carat is still used as such for the weight of gem stones (1 carat is about 200 mg).

charter in return for taking over government debt incurred during the War of the Spanish Succession.

Unfortunately, the charter involved lands owned by Spain, and, although the company did manage one trading venture, that was all that took place. As with the French experience, it was government itself that punctured the boom it had helped create, by passing a law known as the Bubble Act aimed at the kind of joint stock venture that Harley and Blount promoted.

The stock of the South Sea Company rapidly imploded. Blount was nearly killed by angry crowds, and Robert Knight, the company's Treasurer, left for the European continent.

In both these incidents, it is evident that the private sector manipulates the public sector to cause disaster. It is ever thus! Private enterprises seek state favors and then use them to defraud the larger public. Central banking, with its dependence on the state for credibility and viability, is an example of this as well, and offers the same dangers.

BUSINESS CYCLE AND CENTRAL BANKS

One of the main ways that central banks distort the economy and then generate financial mayhem is through the so-called business cycle. The business cycle is likely a natural economic phenomenon. Some sector of the economy becomes popular and products, services and investments boom. Then as the sector is oversupplied, prices slump and a "bust" of some proportion occurs. Absent a central bank, these booms and busts occur regularly and mildly in different business sectors and just as importantly in different geographical locations. This means that while

one area is undergoing a slump another area is in the throes of a resurgence, offering jobs and wealth to those nimble enough to make a business or geographical transition.

But once a central bank has been introduced into the scene, the kinds of booms and busts that would normally affect an economy become regularized and magnified. The central bank issues money for the whole region or country. And because there is no honest money to "govern" the money generation, the issuance of money and credit continues until a downturn becomes not only inevitable, but also far worse than it would have been absent the central bank.

With honest money, the market itself provides a self-limiting mechanism. If too much silver or gold is being circulated, then the value of honest money drops and mines begin to produce less. But once a central bank begins to print money, the invisible hand of

the marketplace is removed and the central bank will certainly overprint on a regular basis. Not only that, but once a boom has turned into a bust, the central bank will likely print even more money to try to rejuvenate the economy. The motor continues to run, with evermore money and credit being supplied.

US Began Without One

It was for this reason, that the United States was founded without a central bank. The founders, specifically Thomas Jefferson, were most aware of the depredations of central banking and fought hard to ensure that the country was erected without any such banking mechanism. In fact, two US central banks were launched in the late 1700s, but both were effectively shut down, the latter by the populist military man and president Andrew Jackson.

One founder, Alexander Hamilton, could not have been pleased with the anti-banking mentality of some US founders, for he was of the school that believed the United States needed a strong central bank as well as a strong centralized government to run a robust monetary policy. Hamilton and others who believed in the European formulation for America even believed that a national debt was a "blessing" because it demanded increased money issuance that supposedly stimulated the economy.

While this is a common justification for central banking, we have already discussed why it is not an accurate one. Ultimately, central banks, untrammeled by market forces,

Ultimately, central banks, untrammeled by market forces, always print too much money and issue too much credit. Hamilton was wrong and Jefferson was right.

always print too much money and issue too much credit. Hamilton was wrong and Jefferson was right.

An "agrarian republican," Jefferson was deeply learned when it came to political philosophy, especially the political systems of the ancient Roman and Greeks. He and other agrarian republicans were determined not to repeat the mistakes of previous empires by making the federal government too strong, thus eventually turning a republic into an empire.

CENTRALIZATION OF POWER

Accordingly, the US Constitution enumerates only the powers that the federal government has received from the states and it is fairly clear to anyone who studies the document that it was the states, not the federal government, who held the balance of power in

the initial relationship between state and federal authority. Senators were to be elected from state legislative bodies and this was done until an amendment changed the procedure to direct elections at the turn of the 20th century. The writings of various Founding Fathers consistently refer to "these united States" a phrase that reflects a voluntary association of states, not an individual super state bound together by a federal authority.

It was only after the Civil War that the balance between the states and federal government changed. Once the North had won the war, it was clear that states did not have the right to secede from the federal government, or at least that the remaining US central power would not let this occur. Lacking the ability to secede, states had no real way of enforcing independence from federal mandates. Post Civil War, the history of the United States has been one of

increasing centralization of power.

It was at this time that the judiciary began to give the federal government more power as well, reinterpreting the commerce clause in the Constitution, giving the federal government the right to regulate interstate commerce, to define interstate commerce as in such a way as to give the federal government the ability to enforce its will on almost any aspect of legislation.

Today, the federal government administers a budget of some $3 trillion based on a gross national product of $12 trillion or more. What this means is that one out of every four dollars spent is in some way influenced by political interests and thus in some way redistributed.

Just as importantly, private bankers under the "color" of the federal government run monetary policy. Until the 20th century,

Today, the federal government administers a budget of some $3 trillion based on a gross national product of $12 trillion or more.

thanks in large part to agrarian republicans like Thomas Jefferson, the United States did not have a federally run monetary system in the European sense of the word. There was no central bank and no graduated income tax. Levers that are common to monetary policy today were thus nonexistent.

All this changed early in the 20th century when, after numerous tries, bankers and industrialists were able to create a central bank and have it rubber-stamped by the US Congress. Also, early in the 20th century, the states ratified a change to the Constitution allowing the federal government to levy a graduated income tax, an ability that resulted in the formation of the IRS and the tax code with all its complexity today.

THE FED ARRIVES

The Federal Reserve system was

actually born of a mysterious conclave that took place on South Carolina's Jekyll Island in a hunting mansion owned by J.P. Morgan. The great industrial and financial magnate along with members of the Rockefeller family and other influential industrialists actually donned disguises to ensure that they were not identified on the train as they traveled down to the hush-hush summit where they developed what would eventually become the Federal Reserve. It was actually these industrialists' third try at passing such a bill. Adding to the intrigue, the bill was submitted for vote in a hurry and passed on Christmas Eve, late at night by the Congress. Critics have been complaining ever since.

Today, when we examine the Federal Reserve from a laissez-faire standpoint we can generate the same kind of questions about the Fed that we would about a European central bank. First of all the Fed is apparently owned

by shareholders, though who these shareholders are seems to be a great controversy — with some at the Fed denying that shareholders exist at all and others pointing fingers at various potential shareholders, powerful families in both America and England.

Why is the issue of shareholders important? Because the mechanism of the Fed is absolutely astonishing when set down in plain English: The Fed, a private corporation, apparently with shareholders, and consisting of representatives from money center banks around the nation, has the authority and duty to print money and create credit for its member. The Fed does not do this by discovering gold and putting it in circulation but simply by authorizing money with a keystroke, literally creating a credit for itself and a debit for the US government and for its citizens.

To put it even more simply: every dollar in circulation today is merely a paper debit created out of thin air. And because the Fed has legally been given the mandate to create this debt, every dollar that the Federal government spends is a dollar more that it owes the private corporation that owns the Fed!

THE FED, TODAY

Why was a federal income tax created at around the same time as the American central bank was set up? Some would argue that those who were doing the lending at the Federal Reserve wanted to make sure that that the US government had revenue coming in to pay for some of the dollars it was borrowing from the Fed.

In any event, the Federal Reserve today is owed trillions of dollars because it has lent

the US trillions of notes that the US pays interest on to the Federal Reserve on annual basis. Some call this sort of system debt-based in that no money can be put in circulation that does not include some sort of debt repayment to the central bank. This is the system that has taken root around the world and almost entirely squeezed out the age-old gold-coin standard as the 21st century advances.

Notice how different this sort of system is from the one that the United States originally started with. A gold-coin economy was based on individuals digging up gold and taking that gold to the US mint to ensure that it was stamped properly and weighed the correct amount when it was turned to coin. Today, an individual cannot go to a US mint to get gold turned to coin. In fact, shockingly, US mints are busy turning out what previous generations would call slugs, lacking almost all

precious metal content. Again, what is happening in the US is happening around the world.

As in other countries, the United States has trouble minting coins that the public will accept beyond what has already been established. One of the most recent coins, coated to look like a gold coin, was roundly rejected and it is possible that institutional memory plays a part in this kind of rejection. People know intrinsically that what the US mint turns out today is far less valuable than what it was set up to accomplish.

Perhaps the most important point in the evolution away from gold to a debt based central banking system in the US and abroad is that a gold-based money system is self-regulating. When there is too much gold in circulation, people cease to dig it up. When there is too little, people dig more.

Do many individual investors purchase silver?

Last year (2006) saw the emergence of investors as net buyers of silver, for the first time since 1990.

Perhaps the most brilliant of these central bank apologists is John Maynard Keynes, himself a central banker.

There is no such self-regulating system when it comes central banking. And this is ultimately why central banking can be, potentially, a destabilizing monetary system. As Murray Rothbard has observed, central banks inflate on a regular basis. Germany learned about central bank inflation before the World War II. More recently Asian and South American countries have learned the hard lesson that fiat money, unhampered by any relationship to gold is money that may well become worthless or at least worth less.

Throughout the 20th century, the dollar functioned as a veritable reserve currency, performing much the same function that gold once performed for the world's financial community. But as we reach the 21st century, the dollar's dominant position may be eroding. Whether central bankers can continue to provide "stability" in a fiat-money world with no dominant currency is certainly an important question. But in order to understand what is to come, we need to examine how modern finance evolved in the 20th century, how the United States came to play such an important role in world finance and why this role is bound to change in the 21st century.

In order to understand the important role that the United States played in 20th century geopolitics it is necessary to understand the evolution of the marketplace that is the United States.

HONEST MONEY REPRESSION

In this chapter, we will deal directly with depredations on gold and silver, with an emphasis on modern ones — a frame of reference that is important for those who wish to understand the value of honest money and its near-term prospects.

Let's take gold first. Gold is highly undervalued today. In 1945, 63,570 tons of gold were available worldwide. In 2003, there were 144,092 tons, a 127% increase. Almost all gold that is mined still exists, as, unlike silver, it is not used much for industrial purposes. In 1945, 68% of all gold was in central bank vaults. In 2003, 12% of all gold was in central bank vaults. The total outstanding value of gold outside bank vaults in 2003 was about 100 times the total

outstanding value of gold outside bank vaults in 1945.

As pointed out by Wall Street analyst Edgar J. Steel in an article, *Golden Escape Pods*, in 1945, the total money in circulation throughout the world was about $300 billion. In 2003, the total money in circulation throughout the world was about $30 trillion, a one-hundredfold increase, which itself suggests a proper price for gold in the area of $3,500 per ounce (100 x $35). Steel adds,

Expressed as a pro-rata portion of the total money in circulation in 1945, each ounce of gold then in existence accounted for $147.48. Expressed as a pro-rata portion of the total money in circulation in 2003, each and every ounce of gold then in existence accounted for $6,506.26. In other words, our money has been robbed of 90% of its value in the last fifty years by excessive expansions of the money supply, with most of the loss taking

Where in the world is all the gold?

Much of the gold is in the form of gold bars, coins and jewellery. Gold bars are often to be found stored in Bank vaults. One of the biggest vaults is Fort Knox in Kentucky, USA which contains the US government's gold reserves. At one time, it held over 22,000 tonnes, but now contains about 8,000 tonnes gold.

place in just the last 30 years. Meanwhile, the per-capita supply of gold actually has declined by about 40%. What's the problem, you might ask — after all, gold went up from $35 to $330 in the same time period, approximately the amount of inflation. Here's the problem: at both points, the price of gold was being artificially constrained by the central bank, both directly and through its surrogate, the American government."

Steele's conclusion about the past century is that "Expressed as a pro-rata portion of the total money in circulation in 2003, each and every ounce of gold then in existence accounted for $6,506.26."

SILVER AND GOLD RATIOS

Given Steele's perspective, you might wonder why gold isn't more popular! Silver, too. Silver tends to trade in a ratio with gold

that has been historically about 16 to one. Today, as of this writing, silver trades around $15 per ounce — a ratio of approximately 60 to one. This means that silver has much farther to climb, probably making it an even better investment than gold which, as of this writing is priced over $800 an ounce.

Back in 1980, silver reached an all time dollar high of nearly $50, which, with the price of gold near $800, put it almost exactly at a 16/1 ratio. We can see that both gold and silver have a long way to go to reach historical pricing averages. The question we want to ask in this chapter is "why?"

There has seemingly always been tension between those who hold gold and those who hold power. Power, after all, is only a tool of those who hold it. There is always something to be gained by holding power, and that something is riches.

> *What would happen to the price of silver in a monetary crisis?*
>
> You could not put a price on silver in a true monetary panic. It would be very high because the markets for both markets are so small.

Those who hold power are in the business of gaining wealth but often once power has been obtained the money-gathering must take place within some sort of quasi-legal environment. Thus the power conundrum — the exercise of power, unless one is prepared to exercise total tyranny, must be subtle and wealth-gathering must not incite the passion of the mass of the citizenry.

Gold and silver, being market money metals — valued by the market and circulated by merchants — have always been resistant to state exploitation. Thus, states have had to refine the ways in which they can manipulate a gold-coin standard

Markets being what they are, the coins were initially valued by the market but soon enough the market valuation became the coins valuation by royal decree.

in order to enrich themselves beyond what would be available through trade or speculation.

COINAGE PRECEDES DEBASEMENT

Kings and emperors unfortunately have tended to build treasuries of gold and silver, too-often based on confiscation and unreasonable taxation. But who knows when it first occurred to an individual in power that he or she could accumulate vast wealth by minting gold coins and placing them in circulation? Probably not long after people began gathering in cities and mass circulation of money became viable.

Markets being what they are, the coins were initially valued by the market but soon enough the market valuation became the coins valuation by royal decree. This set the stage — as we have already pointed out — for

so-called coin shaving, a process by which the state could stamp and put into circulation coins that contained less gold than the coins that were originally valued in the market. The difference in value accrued to the treasury, which then had more gold with which to create more debased coins. By such strategies, the state, and the royal treasury were enriched.

The next breakthrough in the states quest to control money and add to its coffers came through the exercise of war in the 15th century when the very first central bank was created in England to help the Crown pay off war debts.

THE BIG IDEA: THE CENTRAL BANK

The idea of a central bank was very clever, and took the idea of coin shaving to the next level. Prior to central banks being created by the state, the private market had already generated bills circulated in place of gold that were being held in banks and warehouses. However, private banks had to be careful about the bills they circulated because if people got the idea that there was not enough gold in the warehouse to cover the outstanding paper, a bank run could occur that could put the institution out of business.

Central banking came next. We have reported in this book on the invention and rise of central banking and how this took government control of money to a new level. As central banking evolved, bankers and government officials saw that it would eventually allow them to outlaw honest money. It was likely obvious to those who wished to control money for their own purse and profit that eventually central banks could be used to first concentrate and then outlaw honest money.

This is, in fact, exactly what happened, first in Europe and then in America. The American story is especially sad since it was honest money that accounted for much of the rise of America as the most powerful free-market republic that the world has ever seen.

US — POWERFUL FREE-MARKET ENGINE

Free-market proponents would argue that the current situation of these United States has obscured the engine of prosperity that drove one country with less than 5% of the world's population to generate up to 50% of the worlds wealth, revenue and medical and engineering inventions. The foundation for the entrepreneurial culture and ongoing prosperity of the United States was generated (mostly) pre-Civil war days, so this argument goes, and the ability of its citizens to participate freely in the marketplace has been eroding ever since.

Young people, growing up in a wealthy and powerful society are to be excused for their confusion at the beginning of the 21st century. With no firsthand experience of the mostly pre-Civil War industrial miracle that vaulted the United States into a preeminent position in world markets, these young individuals can easily adopt a belief that the historic US configuration is responsible for the current US position. Yet this is obviously a false assessment of the facts from a laissez faire perspective.

It was not a huge federal government that drove the United States engine of commerce or helped develop Yankee ingenuity. Nor was it the size of the country. Hong Kong, with a similar hands-off approach to the development of market-generated wealth, is much smaller than the United States by many orders of magnitude. No, the common factor between Hong Kong and the

Who owns most gold?

If we take national gold reserves, then most gold is owned by the USA followed by Germany and the IMF. If we include jewellery ownership, then India is the largest repository of gold in terms of total gold within the national boundaries. In terms of personal ownership, it is not known who owns the most, but is possibly a member of a ruling royal family in the East.

United States for a very long period of time was the existence of a laissez faire culture. Individuals had access to the markets and their human action added to the well-being of the populace and the wealth of the community.

One may well ask today if the many silk and cotton mills that adorn the rivers of New England would have been built given today's concern for the environment. The great explosion of industrial might developed in the 18th and 19th centuries might not have occurred given today's concerns with pollution and other industry-negative issues. (If this analysis holds, one might easily question whether the European Union with its heavy union and regulatory burdens will ever become the kind of economic force that the United States was in a more unfettered environment. The socialists in the EU may be fooling themselves about what they can accomplish.)

It is not size, after all, as Russia discovered, that determines economic success but the ability of individuals to work, create and plan for the future in a businesslike way without over-taxation or extreme debasement of money.

MONETARY REPRESSION HURTS ALL

This brings us to the second point when it comes to a free-market analysis of the United States success and that is a monetary one.

The first repression of honest money (silver) took place in the 19th century, and the second (gold) in the early 20th century. These events are noted in the history books but seldom put in their proper context. Though they are treated as disparate and even serendipitous, when correctly recited they actually present a clear picture of how the

American monetary elite gradually replaced coins — specie — with paper bills.

The repression of silver as money took place in 1873 in the United States. Wikipedia explains it as follows: "The Fourth Coinage Act was enacted by the United States Congress in 1873 and embraced the gold standard and de-monetized silver. Western mining interests and others that wanted silver in circulation labeled this measure the "Crime of '73". For about five years, gold was the only metallic standard in the United States."

We also learn from Wikipedia that silver was demonitized elsewhere in the world at roughly the same time.

Free silver supporters often claimed that there was involvement by the British [Bank of England] in the passage of the Coinage Act of 1873. Most often they claimed it was Englishman Ernest Seyd who came to the United States to

secure passage of the measure through means of bribe. In February of 1874, Seyd divulged his involvement to a friend at a dinner, and he was sworn to secrecy until after Seyd's death. Upon Seyd's death, the man signed a sworn affidavit of what Seyd told him:

"I went to America in the winter of 1872-73, authorized to secure, if I could, the passage of a bill demonetizing silver. It was in the interest of those I represented — the governors of the Bank of England— to have it done. By 1873, gold coins were the only form of coin money...I saw the committees of the House and Senate and paid the money and stayed in America until I knew the [Coinage Act] was safe."

In addition, Bankers' Magazine of August 1878 reports:

"In 1872, silver being demonetized in France, England and Holland, capital of $500,000.00 was raised and Ernest Seyd of

As we can see above, silver was apparently being demonetized around the world, so the idea that it needed to be done in America because of increased silver production seems unlikely.

London was sent to this country (the United States) with this fund, as the agent of foreign bond-holders and capitalists, to effect the same object here, which was accomplished.

THE TRUTH ABOUT SILVER

Silver was demonetized supposedly because newly discovered silver mines in the American West were pumping silver into the economy, devaluing gold and playing havoc with the silver/gold ratio. In fact, as we can see above, silver was apparently being demonetized around the world, so the idea that it needed to be done in America because of increased silver production seems unlikely. Free-market economics shows us that prices likely have certain levels. In the case of silver and gold, the historical price ratio was 16-to-one (16 ounces of silver for one ounce of gold). While these ratios have fluctuated over thousands of years, the chances are that the ratio would have re-established itself sooner or later in the modern market because as surplus silver built up in the economy, mines producing it would have cut back or shut down. The marketplace itself would have taken care of the silver overhang without another "coinage" act. Again, from Wikipedia:

> In the United States, toward the end of the nineteenth century, bimetallism became a center of political conflict. Newly discovered silver mines in the American West caused an effective decrease in the value of money. In 1873 the government passed the Fourth Coinage Act, at the same time as these resources were beginning to be exploited. This was later referred to by Silverites as "The Crime of '73," as it was judged to have inhibited inflation. Instead deflation resulted, causing problems for farmers with large mortgages but who could sell their goods for only a fraction of their post-Civil War price. In addition, improvements

in transport meant it was cheaper for farmers to ship their grain to Europe, and they over-expanded production until there was a glut on the market. The Panic of 1893 was a severe nationwide depression …

If you have read this book closely, you will recall that absent government demands, an economy prefers the use of both gold and silver simultaneously. Not only is silver the "people's money" but the ratio between silver and gold allows users to detect if widespread manipulation of one money metal or the other is taking place.

Until after the Civil War, the American monetary system included the use of both silver and gold, freely circulated. Thanks in large part to agrarian republicans like Thomas Jefferson, the United States did not have a federally run monetary system in the European sense of the word. There was no central bank and no graduated income tax. Levers that are

common to monetary policy today were thus nonexistent. It was only after the Civil War, with New York bankers in their ascendancy that freely circulating gold and silver came under attack.

ATTACKS ON GOLD

The attacks on silver in the 19th century were only a harbinger for what was yet to come in the 20th century. First, bankers and industrialists were finally able to create a central bank in the United States — a private one that putatively operates under the watchful eye of Congress. Also, early in the 20th century, the states ratified a change to the Constitution allowing the federal government to levy a graduated income tax, an ability that resulted in the formation of the IRS and the tax code in all its complexity today.

What the creation of a Fed did initially was to give both England and the United States a lever to manipulate monetary policy. Accordingly, right after the end of the First World War, English and American central bankers agreed that the pound was to be brought back to its position of international pre-eminence and the dollar, which had risen against the pound was to be debased.

Free-market economists maintain that the reason the dollar had risen against the pound was because the English government had borrowed heavily to fight the First World War and thus the English economy was in poor shape. In fact, the price of the pound had dropped drastically relative to the dollar.

In order to lower the value of the dollar, and raise the value of the pound the US Fed embarked on a purposeful monetary expansion. The immediate result of this monetary expansion was the so-called Roaring

20s and the relentless upward momentum of the stock market as dollars found their way to overvalued equities - stocks that kept being bid up as more cheap money poured into the economy courtesy of the Fed.

FROM BOOM TO BUST

The Fed printed an extraordinary amount of money in the 1920s, debasing the dollar and setting off a huge stock market boom in the meantime. All this ended with a crash in 1929, but even with all the difficulties of monetary expansion, the boom and bust of the 1920s could have been dealt with had the Fed not reversed course and apparently

The Fed printed an extraordinary amount of money in the 1920s, debasing the dollar and setting off a huge stock market boom in the meantime. All this ended with a crash in 1929.

Why was a federal income tax created at around the same time as the American central bank was set up?

tightened the money supply in the early 1930s, turning a routine recession into a depression.

Enter president Roosevelt who understood something about monetary policy in a central banking environment and who gradually began to inflate the money supply, first by confiscating gold and then by injecting credit into the economy.

Roosevelt however, was a hugely activist president, and the regulatory and tax policies of his administration counteracted the monetary expansion he was helping to accomplish. It is unfortunate that his fiscal and regulatory recipe was too enthusiastically adopted in Europe - which struggled through a similar depression.

As Japan was to learn in the 1980s and 1990s, monetary expansion without fiscal discipline cannot bring an economy round. This actually makes a great deal of sense since people cannot do business in an over-regulated and over-taxed environment. If people are not able to do business, then certainly they will not be able to utilize the money that the central bank is injecting into the economy.

WORLD WAR II, ONWARD

It would take World War II to bring the American economy back from the Depression of the 1930s. The 1940s and the 1950s saw the US economy snap back further as some of the regulatory policies of the so-called 'New Dealers' slackened and unions became less powerful in terms of everyday work rules.

By the 1970s, another wave of taxation, regulation and monetary stimulation had conspired to weaken the economic drive of the US. So-called

stagflation, a term that indicated inflation without growth, was utilized to describe what was happening in the 1970s. The United States had printed excessive amounts of money to support the war in Vietnam and the resultant inflation was married to increased regulation and taxation. The offspring was a series of recessions that occurred throughout the 1970s.

The 1980s and the advent of Ronald Reagan brought a new discipline to federal government spending in the United States. Reagan slowed the growth of spending and cut taxes while wringing at least some of the inflation out of the economy. The 1990s benefited from Reagan's 1980s fiscal and monetary policy but it will probably become clear to those who look back on the 1990s in the United States regarding monetary policy that Fed chairman Alan Greenspan, for all of

his claims of low inflation was actually gunning the money supply.

Why didn't inflation show up in the United States in the 1990s? Because the rest of the world was willing to buy and save dollars, thus taking them out of circulation. This left the United States in the enviable position of printing a great deal of money that was exported to other investors, both institutional and individual.

In a sense, the US was exporting its inflation but it couldn't last. Many of the dollars found their way back to the United States in the form of stock investments and eventually US markets became extremely overbought. What happened in the 1920s again happened in the late 1990s, a sizeable crash. And in 2007, the long-term effects of gold suppression came home to roost.

In a sense, the US was exporting its inflation but it couldn't last. Many of the dollars found their way back to the United States in the form of stock investments and eventually US markets became extremely overbought.

The economic tipping point for the United States is no longer theoretical. It is a reality today. The country has gone from the world's largest creditor to its greatest debtor; the value of the dollar is sinking; domestic manufacturing is winding down-and these trends don't seem to be slowing.

It is the argument of this book that we have not arrived at this place in time by accident. In fact, It is likely the deliberate effort of elite monetary policy over decades, even hundreds of years.

Factually speaking, Western elites are at war with their citizens. The object is to gain more control and more wealth and to weaken opposition at the same time. The chosen method is to strip you and me of honest money and our ability to gain it.

Does that sound overly conspiratorial? Hopefully, if you have read this book closely, you will not believe that it is. It is important

that you face reality: And the reality is that honest money gives you a chance to surmount the depreciation of currencies that is taking place all around you and that may well increase in the next few years.

TODAY: A PERFECT 'ECONOMIC STORM'

What we face in the United States and elsewhere is nothing less than an economic "perfect storm." It is one, as hard-money financial commentator Peter Schiff explains, that has been brought on by growing federal, personal, and corporate debt, too-little savings, a declining dollar, and lack of domestic manufacturing.

Another hard-money financial advisor, Gabriel Kolko, puts it in perspective this way:

Contradictions now wrack the world's financial system, and a growing consensus exists between those who endorse it and those

who argue the status quo is both crisis-prone as well as immoral. ...

The International Monetary Fund (IMF), the Bank for International Settlements, the British Financial Services Authority, the Financial Times, and innumerable mainstream commentators were increasingly worried and publicly warned against many of the financial innovations that have now imploded. Warren Buffet, whom Forbes ranks the second richest man in the world, last year called credit derivatives — only one of many new banking inventions — "financial weapons of mass destruction." Very conservative institutions and people predicted the upheaval in global finances we are today experiencing. ...

It is impossible to measure the extent of the losses. The final results of this deluge have yet to be calculated. Even many of the players who have stakes in the countless arcane investment instruments are utterly ignorant. The sums are enormous. The present crisis began — it has scarcely ended there — with sub prime mortgage loans in the US, which were valued at over $1.3 trillion at the beginning of 2007 but are, for practical purposes, worth far, far less today. Indirectly, of course, the mortgage crisis has also brought many millions of people into the larger financial world and they will get badly hurt.

What the sub prime market did was unleash a far greater maelstrom involving banks in Germany, France, Asia, and throughout the world, calling into question much of the world financial system as it has developed over the past decade.

Investment banks hold about $300 billion in private equity debts they planned to place — mainly in leveraged buy — outs. They will be forced to sell them at discounts or

> *What is the relationship between the price of silver and supply?*
>
> As silver prices have risen over the past several years, there has been a revival in the amount of silver being traded on the major silver markets of the world.

keep them on their balance sheets — either way they will likely lose.

The near-failure of the German Sachsen LB Bank, which had to be saved from bankruptcy with 17.3 billion euros in credit, revealed that European banks hold over a half-trillion dollars in so-called asset backed commercial paper, much of it in the form of US sub prime mortgages. Failures in America have also caused Europe to face a crisis. The problem is scarcely isolated.

The leading victims of this upheaval are the hedge funds. What are hedge funds? There are about 10,000 and, all told, they do everything. Some hedge funds, however, provided companies with capital and successfully competed with commercial banks because they took much greater risks. Substantial proportions are simple gamblers; some even bet on the weather. Many of those types have lost huge amounts of money, but

funds based on other, more conservative strategies, also lost enormous sums as well. The spectacular failure of Long-term Capital Management in 1998 was also due to its reliance on ingenious mathematical propositions, yet no one learned any lessons from it, proving that appeals to reason as well as experience fall on deaf ears — especially if there is a widespread belief that there is money to be made. ...

We are at the end of an era, living through the worst financial panic in many decades. Now begins global financial instability. It is impossible to speculate how long today's turmoil will last — but there now exists an uncertainty and lack of confidence that has been unparalleled since the 1930s — and this ignorance and fear are themselves crucial factors. The moment of reckoning for bankers and bosses has arrived. ...

GOLD AND WEALTH PROTECTION

Hopefully, you now understand the reasons why honest money needs to be part of your portfolio. In this chapter, we will provide you with options when it comes to transferring from dishonest money into honest money — silver and gold, and examine ways of doing so.

Investors have many choices when it comes to holding precious metals. They can invest in coins, bars, stocks, mutual funds, ETFs and various derivative instruments including gold futures and options. Silver and gold coins, for instance are an option for many who want to take physical delivery of their gold. However, coins are often priced above their true value by dealers and then

sell below what the sellers believe to be their true value.

Silver and gold bullion is bulky to hold and thus investors may not wish to take delivery of the metal. Additionally, buyers of bullion may be surprised to find that the purchase is reported (in the US anyway) to the regulatory authorities. The same goes for coins with the exception of gold coins that predate President Roosevelt's executive order confiscating gold coins.

Was silver once a popular money metal?

Yes, silver was traded alongside gold and was for a long-time known as the 'people's money' because trades-people could afford silver far more easily than gold.

SECURITIZED OPTIONS

Silver and gold futures and options may be attractive to investors since they can purchase relatively large exposure for a low price. The down-side is that major moves can cost additional money or the

This brings us to stocks — both blue chip and junior miners. When the market moves up, precious metals stocks, large and small benefit.

investor is even in jeopardy of losing his or her entire position.

Mutual funds investing precious metals are a broad-based way to play the market in gold stocks. In the early 21st century several gold mutual funds made large upward moves. The downside to such funds is that they may not reflect the actual power of a broad upward move. The best way to leverage this power is to find a successful silver or gold stock.

This brings us to stocks — both blue chip and junior miners. When the market moves up, precious metals stocks, large and small benefit. But a good junior exploration and development company can benefit most of all — especially when investors seeking fast growing mining companies discover those with valuable stockpiles of gold and silver resources and the added upside potential to significantly increase the size of the deposits.

Whether you choose honest money or not, it is our hope that this book has given you more insight into the real value of money and the uneasy relationship between precious metals and the governments who seek to control them.

WEALTH PROTECTION

I have had the privilege of hosting a conference aptly titled, "The Wealth Protection Conference" in the greater Phoenix area for more than ten years. Each year hundreds of concerned people show up to listen to me and other free-market thinkers as we discuss the state of the economy, specifically as it relates to monetary problems.

It seems obvious to many of these free-market thinkers that gold will likely easily surpass US$2,000 an ounce over the next few years, which means it is just getting back to its inflation-adjusted 1980 high of US$850 per ounce. Regardless of whether it eventually goes to US$10,000 an ounce or not, the 'fiat evaporation' process is well underway and rapidly accelerating.

Suggestion: Get out of your US dollar holdings and any other US dollar fixed income paper (bonds, mortgage backed securities, etc) and move into honest money — physical gold and silver. There is no paper currency today that is anywhere near as safe as honest money, as all paper currencies have allowed themselves to become dislocated from real value. And all of them using the US dollar

as a reserve currency are in especially terrible trouble.

The minimum percentage of physical gold and silver to be held is 10% of the overall wealth portfolio — and that is during good economic times. Today I personally hold well in excess of 40% of my liquid wealth in physical gold and silver bullion.

WE CAN BE A RESOURCE

Resource Consultants, my family-owned and operated advisory business, can advise you on how to do this as cheaply and effectively as possible. Be aware that trading in gold and silver leveraged securities can be a disastrous thing to do. There are companies out there preying on people not overly experienced in transferring into honest money. The only

form of physical gold and silver is that which you can touch.

Because of what has happened previously, in 1933, when the US government declared it illegal for Americans to own gold, I suggest that you do not deposit honest money in a bank's vaults or lock boxes.

In a crunch, and one seems to be unfolding as we speak, the powers-that-be will likely utilize every tool in their war chest including confiscation. However, since the likelihood is that the Internet will continue to expand the base of conscious understanding of the fraud, millions more are likely to seek solutions. Many will find out what you are finding out now — although for most it will be far too late.

How to Get Started

When transferring from "fiat" to honest money, be sure to deposit it for safe-keeping where it will be truly safe and protected from those who may wish to confiscate it. Of course, before this happens, grumblings will issue from powerful think tanks like the CFR (Council on Foreign Relations). Such groups will start to blast gold and silver as conduits for illegal and immoral activities. They may even try to align gold with the flow of money to terrorists. The next step would be for legislators to pass laws mandating that everyone holding silver and gold must report these holdings.

Now we all know what this will be about. It will be about confiscation. The majority will support it on an emotional, albeit illogical basis. Honest money will first be reported and then surrendered.

How does a gold mine work?

The gold-containing ore has to be dug from the surface or blasted from the rock face underground. This is then hauled to the surface and milled to release the gold. The gold is then separated from the rock (gangue) by techniques such as flotation, smelted to a gold-rich doré and cast into bars. These are then refined to gold bars by the Miller chlorination process to a purity of 99.5%. If higher purity is needed or platinum group metal contaminants are present, this gold is further refined by the Wohlwill electrlytic process to 99.9% purity.

What will be returned? Paper money. Depreciating fiat bills! It sounds far-fetched but it is not. It happened before — in America in the 1930s.

There are plenty of ways around it. You can prevent this by simply purchasing your gold and silver through a reputable Swiss-based bullion bank. The Swiss are very cognizant of the value of honest money, especially those located in the Zurich region.

And there are many banks that specialize in the purchase and safekeeping of gold and silver. Purchase rates are highly competitive, so you are usually safe when buying gold and silver through any of the traditional Swiss banks. But do be careful. There are a few that have exhibited a tendency to seek profits abroad in markets that may jeopardize their ability to remain truly neutral in times of heavy international pressure, especially from the American government.

Deposit your gold and silver into a stable and traditional Swiss bullion bank that segregates your gold and silver from anyone else's in the bank. It is also important that the bank offer storage in vaults that are not the property of the bank in the event of insolvency. This can keep you from showing up only to find out that your gold and silver are tied up in courts and subject to creditor's claims. It is good to know that most of the Swiss banks are structured this way.

Many of the Swiss banks also offer you the ability to access your gold and silver (honest money) any time you like with a Visa or Mastercard that is linked to your personal bank account.

EXAMPLE OF WEALTH PROTECTION

What do you need to do now? Sit down and be honest with yourself about what your real wealth is. Include real estate. A typical situation might look as follows:

Assets - US Dollars

1. Real estate (Personal home)
$1,000,000

2. Cash deposits (annual living expenses)
$50,000

3. Fixed Income Funds, T-bills, Bonds, etc.
(Wealth protection) $300,000

4. Stocks and Equity Funds (Wealth growth)
$500,000

Item number 1 assumes you own your own home and therefore the stability of that asset is the value you derive from living in it. Do not live beyond your means. If you do, you risk having no roof over your head at all. However, our example assumes you already own your own home.

Item number 2 acknowledges that you need to maintain sufficient short-term holdings of cash to meet regular living expenses. This model assumes that an average cash balance is maintained of approximately US$50,000 and that each pay interval you replenish your short-term reserve and the balance left over is added to either the preservation side of your wealth formula or to the growth side.

In the above example, I would be especially concerned about number 3. When it comes to asset protection that is where I would be most exposed. Here is where I would immediately reduce that holding by at least 2/3rds leaving a back-up cash reserve for

Many of the Swiss banks also offer you the ability to access your gold and silver (honest money) any time you like with a Visa or Mastercard.

item number 1 of about $100,000, which I would hold in other liquid currencies that are likely to appreciate against the US dollar. I would look at countries with significant holdings of real wealth in the ground and a relatively self-sufficient supply of all natural resources, especially water and carbon fuels.

The Canadian dollar would be a great choice. Over the past few years we have watched as the 'Loonie' has appreciated dramatically against the US dollar. At the time of writing the Canadian dollar is valued at more than US$1.07. Also, consider holding the Swiss Franc. Although the Swiss central bank has exhibited some very worrying behavior since it joined the IMF in

The verdict is still out on the entire European Union. The toxicity of the European continent and its widely diverse mixture of cultures make it highly likely that this marriage "ain't lasting too long."

1992, the bastion of banking has always maintained a solid reserve of gold. Recently the Swiss People's Party has regained a significant amount of power and this bodes well for a future that may return Switzerland to a more traditional monetary policy. Either way, it is still a much more preferable currency to either the dollar or the Euro.

Do not be confused by the strength of the Euro. The verdict is still out on the entire European Union. The toxicity of the European continent and its widely diverse mixture of cultures make it highly likely that this marriage "ain't lasting too long."

However, I would still hold some Euros simply because many who are panicking out of US dollars don't really understand what you now know about money so they just turn to what appears to be a safer investment. So here is what to do with line item 3. Open a fully disclosed bank account with a

traditional Swiss bank such as UBS. Then wire transfer the liquidated proceeds of your entire fixed income portfolio to that account. I certainly wouldn't be holding my $300,000 in US dollars once it got there. UBS would offer you the ability to have Canadian dollar, Swiss Franc and Euro dollar accounts — all broken down on account statements with their values expressed in terms of US dollars for your ease of understanding.

I would take approximately $100,000 and split it into thirds or whatever other mix made more sense after conferring with a professional private banker. If you do not feel that your private banker is as knowledgeable about money as you are... switch private bankers. Still not satisfied — find a new bank with private bankers that do understand. It is very important to deal with someone who truly understands money and what options are available. There are excellent Swiss banks

that have been providing this function for literally hundreds of years. They are well known within hard-money circles.

A good private banker will probably suggest you look at money market funds that invest in those currencies and trades amongst various spots on the yield curve to maximize your rate of interest. Make sure the funds do not invest in leveraged credit paper of any kind. It is bad enough that none of the currencies themselves are backed by sufficient amounts of gold and silver. That's leverage enough.

The money market funds should be redeemable at any time as the reason for holding these cash reserves is to back up line item 2 above in case of extended job loss or other emergency crisis out of your control. During such a crisis, you would naturally begin to reduce your lifestyle expenses as much as possible long before item 2 was gone.

This should enable you to stretch what would ordinarily have been good for only one year's worth of living expenses to maybe two or even three years.

PROTECTING THE REST

Now ask your private Swiss banker to transfer the balance of your $300,000 deposit — US$200,000 — into gold and silver bullion for storage in the bank's vaults, probably in a mix of 80% gold and 20% silver. Think of the gold as money socked away for the long haul; think of the silver as money to be used if the system unravels as badly as it did in Austria and Germany between 1919 and 1923 when their paper money fell to its intrinsic value - firewood.

Silver is therefore another form of reserve, In this case, US$40,000 (US$200,000 x 20%) would get you about 2,800 ounces.

That should be more than enough to protect your family, as silver is likely to be the only form of money affordable when the majority of the population is deeply embroiled in crisis. A few ounces of gold may buy a lot of big-ticket items, where a fistful of silver may likely feed your family for a long time.

Back to item 3 and what I would do with the balance of the US$300,000. After deducting the US$100,000 to create a backup liquid reserve that was split amongst the Canadian dollar, the Swiss Franc and the Euro, US$200,000 remained. From that 20%, i.e. US$40,000 was transferred into physical silver, probably mostly in the form of 100 ounce silver bars and one ounce silver coins. The final US$160,000 would purchase physical gold in the form of one-ounce gold coins. A wonderful coin is the .9999 pure gold Austrian Philharmonic. It offers acceptable premiums over spot when

> **How much does a gold bar weigh?**
>
> Gold is made into a large number of different bars of different weights. The most well known are the large 'London Good Delivery Bars' which are traded internationally. These weigh about 400 Troy Ounces, i.e. 12.5 kg/ 27 lbs. Each. Others are denominated in kilogrammes, grammes, troy ounces, etc. In grammes, bars range from 1 g up to 10 kg. In troy oz, from 1/10 tr.oz. up to 400 tr.oz.. Other bars include tola bars and Tael bars.

compared to the other available coins on the market. Also consider Canadian Maple Leafs. But like anything else, supply and demand affects what makes the most sense at the time you are making your transfer.

This is where you can work with a bullion expert at the bank. They are very experienced trading in the physical gold market and they can provide you with several options. Together you can determine what is appropriate.

Mission Accomplished?

We've helped ourselves a good deal with the above moves: We have successfully positioned ourselves with maximum protection against a falling US dollar without sacrificing our daily lifestyle. We have freed our savings from institutions that might see fit to enact currency controls during

heightened monetary crisis limiting our ability to access our paper money at all.

Using the wealth protection strategy above, you are not cut off from your money — on the contrary you will always have instant access to your money via an offshore credit card, which is really a debit card. This allows you instant access anywhere in the world to your money, even if others aren't able to do so as currency controls take effect. And most importantly, you have secured a significant base of honest money — gold and silver — within your portfolio. Now you have real value behind your wealth. You will enjoy upside purchasing power as others watch theirs disappear.

BUILDING WEALTH

As important as it is to preserve existing wealth, so too is it important to seize opportunities to amass wealth. And opportunities such as this do not come along every day for the average investor. I sincerely believe that right now the business cycle is providing anyone with the foresight the ability to reap enormous potential growth in their investment portfolio — likely rewarding many new millionaires who act now.

We have already established that both gold and silver are money — honest money. And we have examined how to preserve wealth. There are many ways to profit from gold and silver's boom throughout the next several years. However, there exists no better way in my opinion than to own shares of

mining companies that have real value backing up their shares — or paper if you will.

Just as the US dollar is not backed by gold or silver, thus the shares of junior and intermediate exploration companies are not either.

For the purposes of this book I will spend only a brief amount of time focusing on exploration companies. I love exploration. I think there is nothing more exciting than owning shares in a junior exploration company that is exploring for gold or silver when they hit the big one. And, yes it does happen!" And it will happen again. The problem is … which one to buy? There are literally thousands of junior exploration companies scouring every corner of the globe in search of the next mother lode and the odds of success are staggeringly low.

> *Alchemy: Can base metals be turned into gold or silver?*
>
> All metal atoms are made of the same building blocks of protons, neutrons and electrons, but in different quantities, so in theory it could be possible to change base metals into gold or silver. In practice, it is achieved only in nuclear reactions, where heavy radioactive metals decay into other lighter elements.

So why do people invest in such high-risk efforts? As always, for excitement and (potentially) big profit. Promoters rev up the engines as they promote the merits of their company's projects and the stock shoots higher. Smart traders sell when they see that happening — as the odds of total success in this business are little more than one in a thousand.

Aggressive traders who have the patience to speculate and trade on results rather than emotion can have fun in this sector. Buy a couple of junior explorers, but make darn sure you aren't getting yourself into a liquidity trap. Don't ever make the mistake of falling in love with the company — even if it's moving up quickly. It can move back down again just as fast.

OK. For the purposes of wealth building strategies, investing in junior

explorers will not be a big part of the plan —
and for many of us, it won't be part of it at all.

The only caveat I will throw in here is
that at the time of this writing there is an
unprecedented amount of money flowing into
the ground as a result of investor interest in
the surging mining markets. Most of this
money is uninformed and new to mining
stock investing, but regardless there is a lot of
it out there. And inevitably there will be a
major world-class discovery that will lead to
what is known as an "area play" — and area
plays can generate major upside moves.

An area play occurs when a company
makes a bonanza strike and suddenly everyone
wants to get in on it. The company that
makes the strike often sees its share price
trade many times more volume than
previously and this is attractive to promoters
and investors alike. Generally speaking mines
don't occur alone. Where there is one there

are often several. And so a mining rush is born.

Consider keeping a little spare cash around for such opportunities because the irrationality of the market in these cases often pushes the values of the early entrants way beyond common sense, However, it may be profitable for those investors savvy enough to get in early along with the companies flocking to the scene. To stay on top of such developments requires time. Pay attention to what's happening in the mining industry. For that I like to subscribe to newsletters written by credible independent mining analysts that devote their entire time to tracking every move that happens. At the back of the book I have provided a list of some of my favorite analysts and their websites for you to check out.

Now on to how to really make money in the gold and silver boom without taking excessive risk, or for that matter hardly any risk at all.

I'm going to tell you about two companies that have literally created currency backed by honest money. How did they do this you ask? Well, it is the simplicity of their understanding of honest money paired with the skills necessary to effect a very smart strategy.

The two companies I will present are different in only one respect. The first, Seabridge Gold Inc., specializes in the acquisition and accumulation of in-the-ground deposits of literally millions of ounces of gold. The second, Silver Standard Resources, focuses on acquiring and accumulating large stores of in-the-ground deposits of silver. Both companies have done something the Federal Reserve has done — except in reverse.

Consider keeping a little spare cash around for such opportunities because the irrationality of the market in these cases often pushes the values of the early entrants way beyond common sense.

The Fed has continuously created new paper money, thus inflating away the underlying value of real or honest money to a point where the intrinsic value of the paper barely any exists any longer,

Both Seabridge and Silver Standard have used their paper — stock certificates — as a means to raise many millions of dollars which they then used to buy large deposits of ("real") money — gold and silver respectively. Subsequently, as a result of their ability to finance transactions to acquire deposits at costs much less than their underlying value, they actually created a currency in their stock certificates.

What a strategy! And it worked well for them because they were early enough in the gold and silver boom to position themselves for the upside of precious metals as the cycle wears on. Now I am going to state one thing right now, both Seabridge and

Silver Standard are undervalued even though thousands of ordinary people have made fortunes already in their stocks. Why? It's simple. Both gold and silver are nowhere close to their 1980 levels of US$850 and US$52 per ounce respectively. Gold for instance, adjusted for inflation, would need to top more than US$2,000 per ounce just to get back to where it was in 1980. But I, like most who've been in this industry for any serious amount of time, believe that the prices of both metals is likely to dwarf the 1980 inflation adjusted levels. Just how high will they go in price relative to the US dollar? My answer is somewhat of a question in and of itself. The real question is "just how low will the dollar go?"

My response is a lot lower than most people think. The reasons are simple — fundamentals. The US has been drained of its productivity. The country has built an over-

regulated state that no longer stimulates new growth. The dollar has been purposefully inflated beyond repair. America's foreign policy has built a growing legion of "retaliationists" determined to stop her intrusions into their lands. But perhaps more than anything else, society is finding out about all of these issues, and an awakening process is happening.

The Internet is spawning an imagination revolution that hasn't been witnessed since the societal-shifting Gutenberg Press. The unregulated 'Net allows common folks to see clearly the truth about honest money and dishonest money. And those who see and are in a position to act are acting and fast. Yet, it has truly only just begun.

The real stampede has not yet arrived, but when it does, look out! Companies that have built real value — stockpiles of in-the-ground money — gold and silver — will literally shoot up in price. Why? Because there are only a few that understand the formula that Seabridge Gold and Silver Standard have successfully acted upon.

The unfortunate thing about those two companies is that they have already been discovered. Their formula is now known. And their stock prices are reflecting the public's overwhelming support for trading out of a depreciating currency into "their" currency. No matter how you cut it, their paper is backed by real money ... lots of it!

But for those two companies the leverage may be gone, at least in terms of the high leverage their stocks provided in the early 2000s when they traded for under US$1 per share. Getting on board at that time, offered the potential for serious leverage.

> **What is the history of honest money?**
>
> Honest money is a term that describes the direct use and circulation of silver and gold — money metals.

Where is the next Seabridge or Silver Standard? It will surface. It is inevitable. The honest money boom is still young. But management must be skilled and experienced. The company must have the necessary financing ability to raise the paper money needed to acquire deposits of real money. If management can do so at discounts to add value in the ground, then you've got "a winner."

ALTERNATIVE 'NET PRESS

American Conservative
Ananova
Anti-State.com
Antiwar.com
Asia Times
Bruges Group
Build Freedom
Capitol Hill Blue
CounterPunch
Democratic Underground
Drudge Report
eLibertarian
Financial Sense Online
Free Market News Network (FMNN)
Freedom News Daily
Free Republic
Freedom's Phoenix
Future of Freedom Foundation
Gold-Eagle
Huffington Post

Information Clearing House
Jewish World Review
Kitco
Le Metropole Cafe
Lew Rockwell
Liberty For All
Mises Institute
Newsmax
Plug Nickel Times
Prison Planet
Propaganda Matrix
Rational Review
Reason Magazine
Rense
Straits Times
Strike The Root
The Independent Institute
The Last Ditch
The Memory Hole
Truthout
Truth About War
VDARE
What Really Happened
World Net Daily
321 Gold

READING LIST

Browne, Harry.
—"How to Profit from the Coming Devaluation"
—"How I Found Freedom in an Unfree World"

Hayek, Friedrich von.
— "Capitalism and the Historians"
— "The Constitution of Liberty"
— "The Counter-Revolution of Science"
— "Law, Legislation, and Liberty"
— "The Road to Serfdom"

Griffin, Ed.
— "The Creature From Jekyll Island"

Maslow, A. H.
— "The Farther Reaches of Human Nature"
— "Toward a Psychology of Being"

Menger, Carl.

— "Principles of Economics"

Mises, Ludwig von.

—"Human Action"

— "Liberalism"

— "Omnipotent Government"

— "Socialism"

— "Theory and History"

— "The Theory of Money and Credit"

Orwell, George.

— "Animal Farm"

— "1984"

Rand, Ayn.

__"The Virtue of Selfishness"

— "Atlas Shrugged"

Rothbard, Murray.

— "America's Great Depression"

— "An Austrian Perspective on the History of

— "Conceived in Liberty"

— "Man, Economy, and State"

— "Power and Market"

— "What Has Government Done to Our Money?"

Wile, Anthony.

—"High Alert"

PAT GORMAN'S BIOGRAPHY

Pat Gorman is a precious metals dealer, well-known radio host and now Chairman of Constitution Mining Corp.

As a hard-money strategist, Mr. Gorman has helped individuals solve the problem of "fiat" money and inflation throughout his career. He believes that precious metals are the ultimate store of value - and that paper money inevitably loses value since more of it is always printed than needed.

For the last 13 years Pat has also run his own radio talk show in Phoenix, AZ called "Hard Money Watch." It has been rated in the top five radio talk shows in Phoenix for the last 10 1/2 years. Listeners can gain access to the show anywhere in the world via the Internet. The show is on at 7:00 a.m. Mountain Standard Time on Sunday mornings at www.KFNN.com.

"The service we provide clients is what has established our business and made us grow," Mr. Gorman points out. "But a large part of what we do today has to do with education and financial literacy — education before acquisition. If the system does collapse, there's no question that precious metals will fill the monetary void as they always have."

SELECT NEWSLETTER WRITERS

Robert Bishop, Hard Rock Advisories, hraadvisory.com
Doug Casey, International Speculator, caseyresearch.com
James Dines, The Dines Letter, dinesletter.com
Cliff Droke, Market Analysis, clifdroke.com
Jason Hommel, Silver Stock Report, silverstockreport.com
Al Korelin, Korelin Economics Report, kereport.com
Brien Lundin, Gold Newsletter, goldnewsletter.com
Richard Maybury, U.S. & World Early Warning Report, chaostan.com
Greg McCoach, The Mining Speculator, gregmccoach.com
David Morgan, The Morgan Report, silver-investor.com
Harry Schultz, The Harry Schultz Letter, hsletter.com
Ron Struthers, Struthers' Resource/Tech Report, playstocks.net
Jay Taylor, J Taylor's Gold & Technology Stocks, miningstocks.com
James Turk, Gold Money, goldmoney.com